Stargold's No-Recipe Recipes

written by **Claudia Lemay, RD**
with illustrations by Chris Hamilton & Chris Kielesinski

Table of Contents

p. 3	Cooking Essentials and Non-essentials
p. 4	Base Recipe - Fried Garlic and Onion
p. 6	No Monkey Vegetable Soup
p. 8	Bricks and Mortar Legume Salad
p. 10	Energy Smoothie
p. 12	Lunch Box Muffins
p. 14	Tool Box Sandwiches & Wraps
p. 16	Super Strength Stir Fry
p. 18	Stargold's Super Spaghetti Sauce
p. 20	Skeleton Grilled Cheese
p. 22	Laser Fruit Skewers & Dip
p. 24	Pilot's Garden Salad
p. 26	Hummus of the Geeks
p. 28	Hannah Banana 'Nice' Cream
p. 30	Monkey's Lunch Banana Pancakes
p. 32	Hearty Shepherd's Pie
p. 34	Lucie's Favourite Chia Seed Pudding
p. 36	Overnight Oats
p. 38	Pete's Pizza
p. 40	Morning Scramble
p. 42	Smart Potion Vinaigrette
p. 44	Strong Muscles Potion Creamy Vinaigrette
p. 46	Iron Water
p. 48	Stargold's Pyramid Nutrition Guide
p. 49	Canada's Food Guide: Stargold's Plate
p. 50	Stargold's Word Finder
p. 51	Stargold's Guessing Game
p. 52	Stargold's Food Chart
p. 53	Stargold's Food Guide
p. 54	Colouring Fun - Growland
p. 56	Colouring Fun - Stargold's Friends
p. 57	Colouring Fun - Active Lucie
p. 58	Meet the Author and the Illustrators

Laying the Foundation

Cooking Essentials

There are several cooking 'essentials' that everyone needs to know about and follow. For example, if someone is making a vegetable soup, they will need some kind of broth and likely a fried onion. These would be considered vegetable soup 'essentials,' and are an example of what children will learn to be able to make with **Stargold's No-Recipe Recipes**. The essentials for various basic meal types are taught. Learning to make recipe 'essentials' will allow kids to be able to prepare food on their own, and not have to always rely on less nutritious and more expensive store-bought convenience foods.

Cooking Non-essentials

The **'non-essentials'** of a dish are up to us. For example, with vegetable soup, once the broth and fried onion are ready, anything else can be used to complete the soup and are thus called the 'non-essentials'. They will depend on what we want to put in the soup, what we feel like eating, and most often, what is in the fridge. Do you have tomatoes? Well then, make tomato soup! Do you have broccoli? Let's make broccoli soup! Do you have some mustard? Hmm...well... please let us know how that turned out!

Meal Preparation

All fruits and vegetables should be thoroughly washed before incorporating into all recipes. All raw meat ingredients should be kept separated from other ingredients. This includes using different cutting boards and utensils. Ask your parents for help if you need to use the stove. Use sharpened but blunt knives when chopping to reduce the risk of cutting your fingers. You have 10 of them, we would rather you keep them all.

Base Recipe

The base recipe will be used often and is referred to in some of the following recipes. It consists of sautéing (fancy word for frying) garlic and onion over medium heat in oil.

Essential: • Oil

Non-essentials: • Onion • Garlic

What to do: Fry onion and garlic in oil for 3 minutes

Bring your creation to life: Colour the foods and utensils below!

Stargold's No-Recipe Recipes

Base Recipe
Sautéed Garlic and Onion

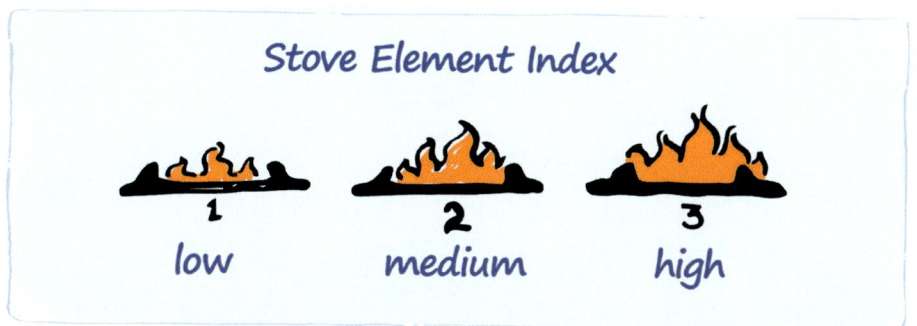

1.

2. Canola Oil

3. 3 min.

2

Stove Element Index

1 low — 2 medium — 3 high

visit: www.stargoldthefoodfairy.com or www.stargoldfoundation.org

No Monkey Soup

Everybody loves soup and it is a wonderful way to use up the vegetables that have been forgotten in the fridge. Tip: Make a great big batch without using any tomatoes. Then, when you have eaten half of it, add a can of tomatoes to get a whole new soup experience. Soup can easily be frozen.

Essentials: • Broth • Onion • Oil • Salt and pepper

Non-essentials: • All the vegetables, herbs and spices you like [Examples: • Carrots • Celery • Tomatoes • Potatoes • Squash • Corn • Broccoli • Green beans • Peas • Legumes, etc.]

What to do: Base Recipe (page 4). Add vegetables and fill the pot with broth. Cook until vegetables are soft.

Bring your creation to life: Colour the foods below!

Stargold's
No-Recipe Recipes

No Monkey Soup
Vegetable Soup

1 Base Recipe (see page 4)

2 Any of these...

+ (carrot, celery, potato, peas, broccoli, legumes) etc.

3 + Broth

or

4 30 min.

Add... (salt, pepper, Herbs, Spices)

visit: www.stargoldthefoodfairy.com or www.stargoldfoundation.org

7

Bricks & Mortar Legume Salad

Legumes are super-duper healthy. They are high in protein and fibre, which will keep your energy levels up for a long time.
Examples of legumes are chickpeas, lentils and beans.

Essentials: • Canned legumes • Onions • Vinaigrette* • Salt and pepper

Non-essentials: • All the vegetables, herbs and spices you like [Examples: • Tomatoes • Carrots • Lettuce • Bell peppers • Cumin • Red chilli flakes • Fresh cilantro]

What to do: Rinse canned legumes with water, drain, add other vegetables and vinaigrette*, mix well and voilà!

*Vinaigrette: See recipe on page 42 or 44

Bring your creation to life: Colour the foods below!

Stargold's
No-Recipe Recipes

Bricks & Mortar
Legume Salad

1 Legumes

2 Any of these...

3

4 Add Vinaigrette
(see page 42 or 44 recipe)

etc.

Add... Herbs Spices

f visit: www.stargoldthefoodfairy.com or www.stargoldfoundation.org

9

Energy Smoothie

"I don't have the time" is NOT a good reason to skip awesome food before going to school. Here is why: it will take you 60 seconds or less to make, if you prepare the ingredients the night before.

Essentials: • Milk (any type) • Juice or Water • Ice (if using fresh or thawed fruit)

Non-essentials: Any fresh/frozen fruit (even vegetables) you want: • Banana • Berries (strawberries, blueberries, raspberries) • Melon (watermelon, honeydew, cantaloupe) • Pineapple • Kale • Orange • Mango • Peach • Celery • Oats • Seeds • Nuts (almonds, peanut butter, pecans, walnuts...)

What to do: Wash and chop up fruit. Put fruit in a blender. Add milk/juice/yogurt/water and blend until smooth.

So quick, it's magic (you will see, the whole thing will take you about 30 seconds)!

Bring your creation to life: Colour the foods below!

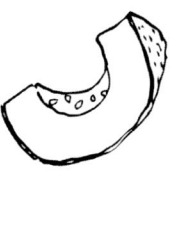

Stargold's No-Recipe Recipes

Energy Smoothie
Smoothie

1.
- Yogurt
- Frozen Fruit
- bananas, apple, blueberries, strawberry, melon, celery, carrot, wheat, seeds, nuts
- etc.

2.
- Ice cubes
- **+**
- Milk or soy
- and/or Juice

3. Blend

visit: www.stargoldthefoodfairy.com or www.stargoldfoundation.org

11

Lunch Box Muffins

Baking is one of the main exceptions to our no-recipe recipes because baked goods need to have exact measurements to rise properly. This recipe will make 12 great muffins. Muffins can be easily frozen to keep them fresh. Pack frozen muffins in your lunch kit, that way, they won't get squished.

Essentials: • 2 cups whole wheat flour • 3 teaspoons baking powder • ½ teaspoon salt • ¾ cup sugar • 1 egg • 1 cup milk • ¼ cup vegetable oil

Non-essentials (Up to 1 cup): Any fresh/frozen fruit you want: • Berries (strawberries, blueberries, raspberries) • Bananas • Apples • Pineapple • Dried fruit (raisins, cranberries) • Nuts (walnuts, almonds, peanuts) • Chocolate chips (Stargold's favourites) • Seeds (pumpkin, hemp, sunflower...) • spices and other flavours (cinnamon, vanilla extract, coconut flakes, poppy seeds, cocoa powder)

What to do:
1. Preheat oven to 400 degrees F (200 degrees C). Line muffin tray with muffin cups.
2. In a bowl, stir the dry ingredients together.
3. In another bowl, beat the egg with the milk and oil. Mix it into the flour mixture.
4. Add up to 1 cup of any of the optional ingredients.
5. Pour into muffin cups.
6. Bake for 25 minutes.

Stargold's No-Recipe Recipes

Lunch Box Muffins
Muffins

1. 400°F / 200°C

2. **Dry Ingredients**
   Whole Wheat — 2 cup + 3 Tsp Baking Powder + 1/2 Tsp S + Sugar 3/4 cup

3. **Wet Ingredients**
   1 cup Milk + 1 egg + 1/4 cup Oil

4. (bananas, blueberries, nuts) — 1 cup

5.

6. 400°F / 200°C

7. 25 min.

visit: www.stargoldthefoodfairy.com or www.stargoldfoundation.org

Tool Box Sandwiches & Wraps

Sandwiches are quick, easy and delicious. Everyone needs to know how to make a good sandwich! Sandwiches can easily be frozen, but leave the mayo and veggies out if you are planning to freeze them. You can make a whole batch of sandwiches on the weekend and then take one out each morning for your lunch.

Essentials: • Tortilla wrap or bread • Mayo • Salt and pepper

Non-essentials: • Mustard • Cheese (cream cheese, grated, sliced) • Cold cuts • Canned tuna • Hummus • Hard-boiled eggs (mashed) • Any fresh/frozen vegetable, Green onion • Avocado • Shredded vegetables (zucchini, bell peppers, lettuce, carrots, etc.) • Any herbs/spices you like (Dill/Basil/Paprika)

What to do: Wash all vegetables and shred them. Spread and lay your ingredients on the whole grain wrap/bread.

Bring your creation to life: Colour the foods below!

Stargold's
No-Recipe Recipes

Tool Box Sandwiches
Sandwiches

1

Mustard

Mayo

2

etc.

Hummus

or

Cold Meats*

Eggs

Tuna

*Cold Cuts are not the greatest. The less you eat the better.

visit: www.stargoldthefoodfairy.com or www.stargoldfoundation.org

Super Strength Stir Fry

A tasty, basic dish that allows us to incorporate lots of awesome colours and flavours in our meals.

Essentials: • Cooking oil • Soy sauce • Sesame oil

Non-essentials: • Meat (chicken/beef/veggie ground) • Firm tofu • Any fresh/frozen vegetable, herbs or spices you like [Examples: Carrots • Peas (snow peas, snap peas) • Green beans • Corn • Broccoli • Zucchini • Onions / Green onions / Shallots • Bell peppers • Mushrooms • Water Chestnuts • Cauliflower • Bean sprouts]

What to do: Base Recipe (page 4). Fry meat or tofu in oil and cook until done. Add soy sauce and other vegetables and cook until soft. Toss with sesame oil to finish and serve on whole grain noodles or brown rice.

*Stir fry leftovers can easily be frozen.

Bring your creation to life: Colour the foods and utensils below!

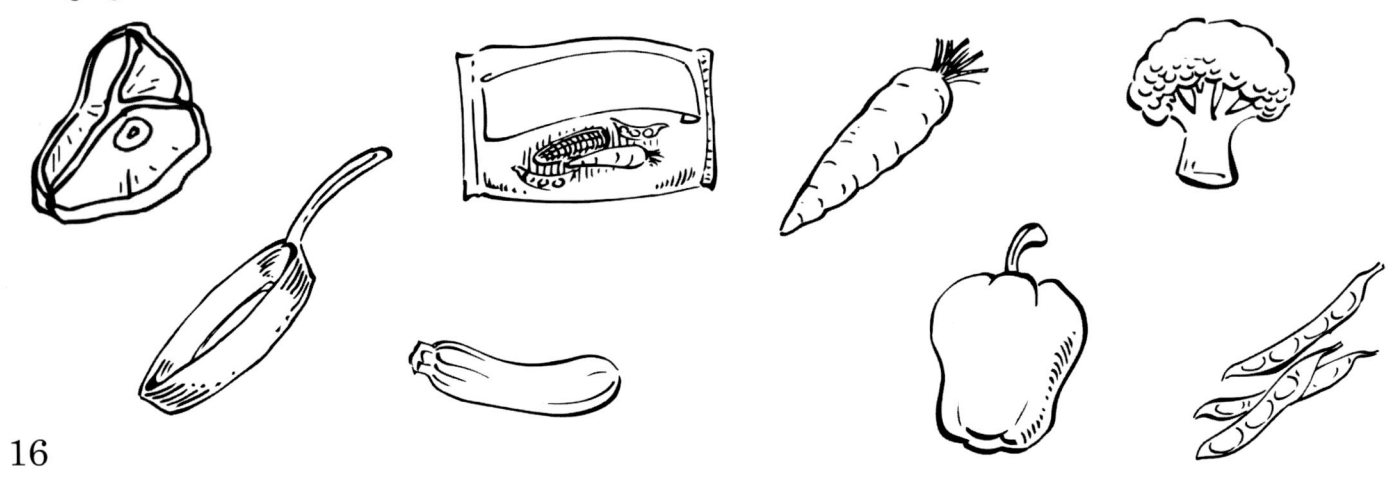

Stargold's No-Recipe Recipes

Super Strength
Stir Fry

1. Base Recipe (see page 4)

2. Add — chicken or steak or Veggie Ground or Tofu

3. Cook until brown

4. Any of these... zucchini + carrots, broccoli, green beans, bell pepper, mushrooms, etc. Vegetables

5. 5 min

6. Canola Oil, Sesame Oil

7. rice or noodles

Add... Herbs, Spices

3

visit: www.stargoldthefoodfairy.com or www.stargoldfoundation.org

17

Stargold's Super Spaghetti Sauce

Another good basic recipe – everyone eats spaghetti! Once you make this, your parents, and YOU, especially, will be very proud. The sauce can easily be frozen. Freeze in quantities appropriate for one meal.

Essentials: • Ground beef/turkey/tofu or any meat alternative • Canned tomatoes • 1 Onion • Garlic • Olive oil • Salt and pepper

Non-essentials: All the vegetables, herbs and spices you like [Examples: Bell pepper • Carrot • Zucchini • Mushrooms • Italian herbs (Basil, Oregano, Thyme)]

What to do: Base Recipe (page 4). Add ground beef or veggie meat and cook until brown. Add tomatoes, vegetables and herbs. Cook until soft and serve on whole grain pasta.

Bring your creation to life: Colour the foods below!

Stargold's No-Recipe Recipes

Stargold's Super Sauce
Spaghetti Sauce

1 Base Recipe (see page 4)

2 + Ground or or Veggie Ground or Tofu

3 Cook until brown

4 + (vegetables) etc.

5 + (canned tomatoes)

6 + Herbs Spices

7 Cook for 30 min

visit: www.stargoldthefoodfairy.com or www.stargoldfoundation.org

19

Skeleton Grilled Cheese Sandwich

So easy, so good. Remember: the better the cheese you use, the better your sandwich will turn out. Serve with a big salad and you will have a great meal.

Essentials: • Sliced whole grain bread • Soft butter/soft margarine • Cheese

Non-essentials: • Tomato • Ham • Dijon mustard • Diced onions

What to do: Put butter on one side of the slice of bread. Turn upside down. Put cheese and optional ingredients on top. Add another slice of bread and butter the top. Cook in a frying pan over medium heat until the cheese is melted and each side of the bread is golden brown.

Bring your creation to life: Colour the foods and utensils below!

Stargold's No-Recipe Recipes

Skeleton Grilled Cheese
Grilled Cheese Sandwich

1.
2.
3. +
4. Any of these... etc.
   - Dijon Mustard
5.
6. flip when brown

2

visit: www.stargoldthefoodfairy.com or www.stargoldfoundation.org

Laser Fruit Skewers & Dip

Skewers make eating fruit really good and really fun - So much better than cotton candy or marshmallow stew, really.

Essentials: • Fruit • Skewers • Yogurt

Non-essentials: • Honey • Lemon juice • Vanilla extract • Cinnamon • Cream Cheese • Cream • Chocolate

What to do: Put fruit on skewers. Dip in the mix of yogurt and optional ingredients.

Bring your creation to life: Colour the foods and utensils below!

Stargold's No-Recipe Recipes

Laser Fruit Skewers & Dip

1. Lemon or HONEY or Vanilla Extract or Cinnamon or Cream Cheese or Chocolate — 1 Cup Yogurt

2. Chopsticks + knife — bananas, strawberry, melon, pineapple, etc.

3. Skewer the fruit

4. Mix and dip

visit: www.stargoldthefoodfairy.com or www.stargoldfoundation.org

Pilot's Salad

Salad is a true essential. Don't get caught using only lettuce, tomatoes and cucumber every day though! You will quickly get very bored of that. Use a good dressing and put fun stuff in your bowl as well: good food tastes good!

Essentials: • Salad greens • Salt and pepper

Non-essentials: • All the vegetables, legumes, herbs and/or spices you like [Examples: Onions • Avocado • Bell pepper • Shredded Carrot or Beet • Radish • Kale • Tomato • Cucumber] • Other fun stuff [Examples: Berries • Orange • Pomegranate • Nuts (almonds, walnuts, candied pecans) • Dried fruit and seeds (hemp, flax, sunflower)]

What to do: Add any chopped vegetables to your salad greens. Pour vinaigrette on the salad only after they have been served. That way, the salad won't end up all soggy and you will have left overs for the next day.

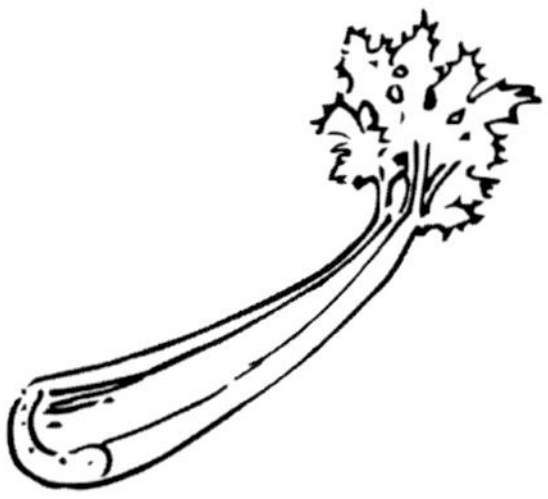

*Vinaigrette: See recipe on page 42 or 44

Bring your creation to life: Colour the foods and utensils

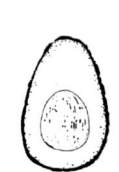

Stargold's No-Recipe Recipes

Pilot's Salad
Garden Salad

1.

2. Any of these...

or Kale, Radish

3. Fun stuff...

Berries, Oranges, Pomegranate

Nuts: Almonds, Walnuts

Dried Fruits & Seeds: Hemp, Flax, Sunflower

4. Add Vinaigrette (see page 42 or 44 recipe)

visit: www.stargoldthefoodfairy.com or www.stargoldfoundation.org

Hummus of The Geeks

Hummus can be used in billions of ways. You can use it as a dip for your carrot sticks, a salad dressing, a sandwich filling, or a treat to devour by the spoonful. Ice cream Hummus, why not? Go wild!

Essentials: • Cooked Chickpeas • Tahini • Lemon Juice • Olive Oil • Garlic • Salt

Non-essentials: • Other cooked vegetables (beets, peas, red peppers, sundried tomatoes, etc.) • Spices (cumin, paprika, turmeric, etc.)

What to do: Rinse and drain the cooked chickpeas. Blend all ingredients in food processor until smooth.

Bring your creation to life: Colour the foods and utensils below!

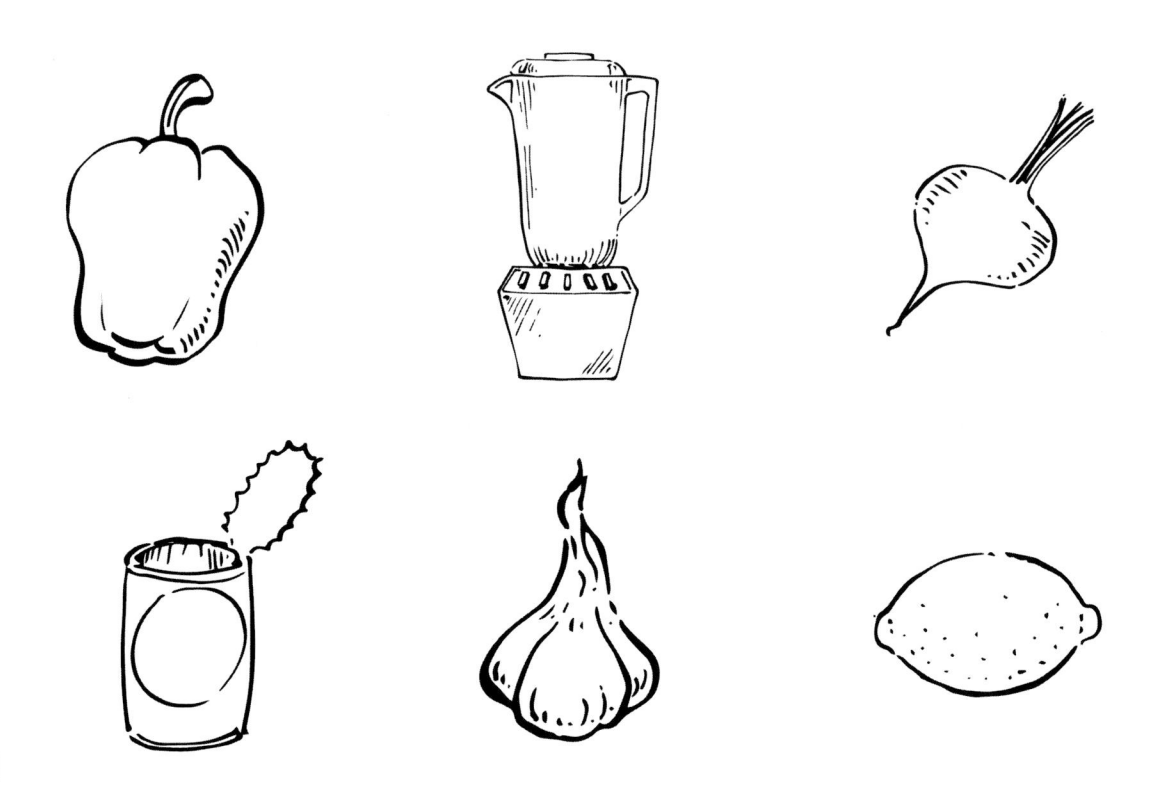

Stargold's No-Recipe Recipes

Hummus of the Geeks
Hummus Dip

2

tahini — 1/4 Cup

1/4 de tasse — Olive Oil

Chick Peas   Chick Peas

3

Blend Until Smooth

You may need to add water

Add... Herbs Spices

visit: www.stargoldthefoodfairy.com or www.stargoldfoundation.org

27

Hannah Banana 'Nice' Cream

Nice ice cream that everyone will love! It will give you energy and lots of tools to build your body.

Essentials: • Frozen Bananas • Milk or yogurt

Non-essentials: • Cocoa powder • Vanilla • Berries or any other fruit (mangoes, peaches, oranges, etc.)

What to do: Peel ripe bananas. Slice into wheels. Freeze. Blend frozen bananas and other ingredients you wish to have in the food processor/blender until smooth.

Bring your creation to life: Colour the foods and utensils below!

Stargold's No-Recipe Recipes

Hannah Banana
Nice Cream

1 Frozen Bananas (peel and slice before freezing)

2
- Frozen Fruit
- Yogurt*
- Milk*
- Juice*

*splash of

3 [blender]

visit: www.stargoldthefoodfairy.com or www.stargoldfoundation.org

Monkey's Lunch Banana Pancakes

Who said pancakes were only for breakfast? Serve it with fruit and a glass of milk (soy or cow for a complete nutritious meal). A Body Builder Elf worthy meal!

Essentials: • 1 cup whole wheat flour • 1 tablespoon sugar • 1 tablespoon baking powder • Pinch of salt • 1 cup soy milk or yogurt • 1 banana • Splashes of oil

Non-essentials: • Cocoa powder • Vanilla • Berries or any other fruit (Mangoes, peaches, chocolate chips, etc. YES, chocolate chips are a fruit)

What to do: Mix dry ingredients into bowl. Add milk, oil and non-essential ingredients. Mix and then spoon mixture into oiled hot pan. Flip once you see bubbles or the edges start to brown. Repeat until mixture is all gone!

Bring your creation to life: Colour the foods below!

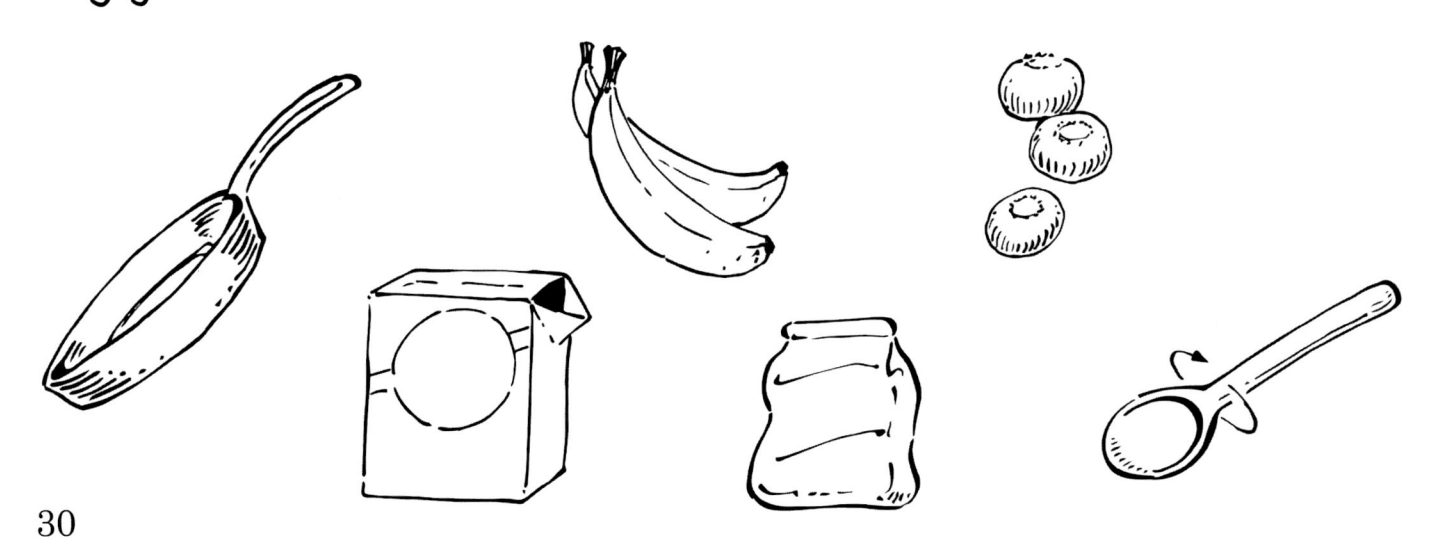

Stargold's No-Recipe Recipes

Monkey's Lunch
Banana Pancakes

1. Dry Ingredients

Whole Wheat → 1 Cup + 1 tbsp Baking Powder + 1 tbsp Sugar + 1/2 Tsp Salt

2. Wet Ingredients — smashed —

1 Cup Soy Milk, bananas, Canola Oil

3. 1/2 Cup (nuts, blueberries)

4. Canola Oil in pan, cook over fire.

visit: www.stargoldthefoodfairy.com or www.stargoldfoundation.org

31

Hearty Shepherd's Pie

Good memories from Stargold's childhood! Stargold used to add a ton of ketchup, mix it all together to make a huge mountain of pink mushy yummy stuff and ate it with a spoon.

Essentials: • Ground veggie meat or ground beef • Potatoes • Corn • Olive Oil • Milk • Onion • Garlic • Salt and Pepper

Non-essentials: • Other cooked vegetables or beans (carrots, peas, lentils) • Seasoning (steak spice, paprika, parsley, chili flakes, onion salt, garlic salt, etc.)

What to do: Base Recipe (page 4). Add ground veggie meat or ground beef, add non-essential veggies and seasoning. Pour into oven safe dish. Pour a layer of corn on top of the meat. Cook potatoes in salted boiling water until soft. Drain, mash, add milk, butter (or margarine) and seasoning and pour on top of the corn. Bake in oven (425 degrees F / 225 degrees C) for 10 minutes or until potatoes are brown on top.

Bring your creation to life: Colour the foods and utensils below!

Stargold's No-Recipe Recipes

Hearty Shepherd's Pie

1. Base Recipe
2. ➕ Ground or Veggie Ground
3. Corn
4. Peel & Chop — H₂O, 10 min
5. (drain)
6. MASH! — Soy Milk
7. 425°F / 225°C, 10 min

visit: www.stargoldthefoodfairy.com or www.stargoldfoundation.org

Lucie's Favourite Chia Seed Pudding

Chia puddings are full of good stuff for your brain, for your muscles, for your belly and for your tongue.

Essentials: • 1/3 cup Chia seeds • 2 cups soy milk or milk

Non-essentials: • Cocoa powder • Vanilla • Berries or any other fruit (mangoes, peaches, oranges, etc.) • Maple syrup • Cinnamon

What to do: Mix chia seeds with milk or soy milk. Shake well. Place in fridge overnight or wait at least 4 hours before adding non-essential ingredients. Mix and devour!

Bring your creation to life: Colour the foods and utensils below!

Stargold's No-Recipe Recipes

Lucie's Favourite Chia Seed Pudding

1 Chia / Milk

2 Shake! Shake! Shake!

3 4hrs or Overnight

4 (cherries, blueberries, raspberries, peach, bananas, nuts, Frozen Fruit, coconut)

1/4 Chia

visit: www.stargoldthefoodfairy.com or www.stargoldfoundation.org

35

Overnight Oats

You don't have to rely on mom or dad for your breakfast anymore. By preparing something at dinner time, you can choose the stuff that will go into it. Strawberries ✓ check, chocolate chips ✓ check, walnuts ✓ check, brussel sprouts and wasabi ✗ NO WAY! Now you will have something delicious to look forward to when your alarm clock goes off on school days.

Essentials: • Oats • Soy milk or cow milk

Non-essentials: • Cocoa powder • Vanilla • Berries or any other fruit (banana, mangoes, peaches, oranges, etc.) • Maple syrup • Cinnamon • Coconut

What to do: Fill container half way with oats. Pour in the milk. Cover. Go to bed. In the morning, add the fun stuff (non-essentials)

Bring your creation to life: Colour the foods and utensils below!

Stargold's No-Recipe Recipes

Overnight Oats

1 Oats / Milk

2 Bananas, blueberries, strawberries, peach, peanuts, coconut

3 4hrs or Overnight

1/3 Oats

visit: www.stargoldthefoodfairy.com or www.stargoldfoundation.org

37

Pete's Pizza

What kid does not love pizza? A favorite for kids of all ages, even mom and especially dad.

Essentials: • Whole wheat pita bread • Tomato sauce • Grated cheese • Olive oil

Non-essentials: • You • know • What • Goes • On • Pizza

What to do: Drizzle olive oil on pita. Spread tomato sauce and cover with cheese. Tada!

Bring your creation to life: Colour the foods and utensils below!

Stargold's No-Recipe Recipes

Pete's Pizza

1.
2.
3. etc.
4. 400°F / 200°C

visit: www.stargoldthefoodfairy.com or www.stargoldfoundation.org

Morning Scramble

People often say that breakfast is the most important meal of the day. Both Stargold and Lucie love breakfast, as it provides such an awesome start to their day! Morning scrambles are quick and super easy to make. Since they are high in protein, it makes them a great source of energy to last you until lunch.

Essentials: • Crumbled firm tofu or eggs • Olive oil • Onion • Garlic • Salt and pepper

Non-essentials: • Other cooked vegetables (bell peppers, mushrooms, sundried tomatoes, etc.) • Grated cheese • Black beans • Spices (cumin, paprika, turmeric, chipotle, nutritional yeast, etc.)

What to do: Base Recipe (page 4). Fry non-essential vegetables, add tofu or eggs and seasonings, mix and cook for 5 minutes. Serve with avocado, potatoes, toast, tomatoes and/or salsa. Place into a flour or corn tortilla for an awesome breakfast burrito.

Bring your creation to life: Colour the foods and utensils below!

Stargold's No-Recipe Recipes

Morning Scramble

1 Base Recipe (see page 4)

2 [knife, mushroom, green pepper, tomato, can of Beans] etc.

3 Add... Salt, Pepper, Herbs, Spices

4 Crumbled Tofu or Eggs

5 [grater and cheese]

10 min

visit: www.stargoldthefoodfairy.com or www.stargoldfoundation.org

Smart Potion Vinaigrette

Healthy oils are a must to help us grow smart and healthy. Using good oils for all your salads and marinades is a great way to provide your brain with the building blocks it needs for its development.

Essentials: • Olive oil • Vinegar (white, balsamic, cider) • Garlic • Dijon mustard • Salt and pepper

Non-essentials: • Honey • Herbs/spices • Lemon juice

What to do: Fill a jar to one-third with vinegar and/or lemon juice. Chop garlic and add other ingredients (except oil) and mix very well with lid tightly closed. Then, fill another one-third of the jar with oil and close the lid. Mix again.

Bring your creation to life: Colour the foods and utensils below!

Stargold's
No-Recipe Recipes

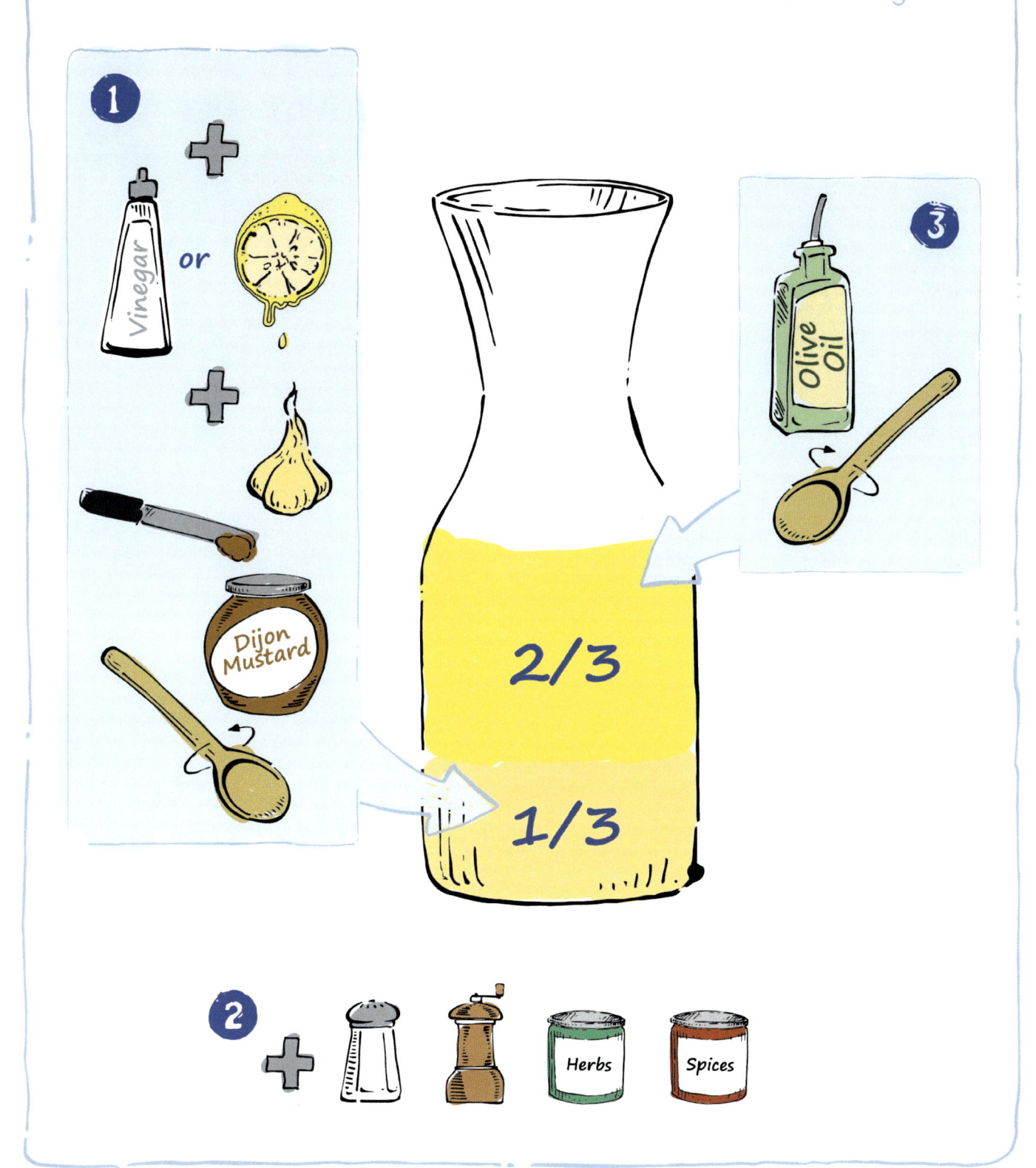

Smart Potion
Vinaigrette

1
- Vinegar or Lemon
- +
- Garlic
- Dijon Mustard

2
- + Salt, Pepper, Herbs, Spices

3
- Olive Oil

2/3 Olive Oil
1/3 Vinegar/Lemon mix

visit: www.stargoldthefoodfairy.com or www.stargoldfoundation.org

Strong Muscles Potion Creamy Vinaigrette

This vinaigrette is good for salad and it is good for sandwiches as well (eg. egg salad sandwiches). It's also good for your muscles and for your bones.

Essentials: • Mayo • Greek yogurt (2%) • Garlic • Mayo • Lemon juice / Zest • Salt and pepper

Non-essentials: • Herbs/spices

What to do: Fill a jar half-way with mayo. Add lemon juice/zest, crushed garlic, salt and pepper and mix together. Then add yogurt and mix all together.

Bring your creation to life: Colour the foods and utensils below!

Stargold's
No-Recipe Recipes

Strong Muscles Potion
Creamy Vinaigrette

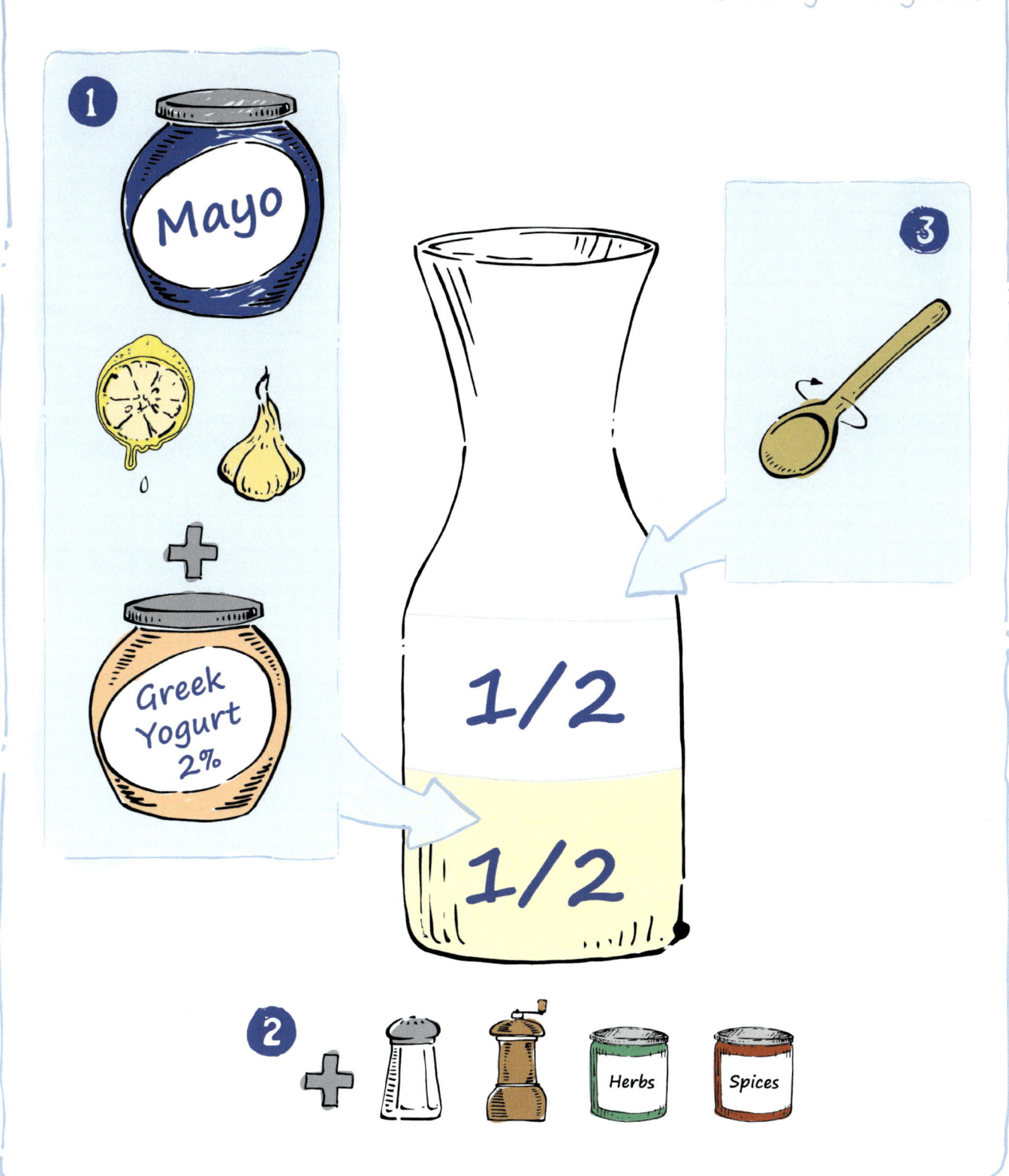

1
- Mayo
- Lemon
- Garlic
+
- Greek Yogurt 2%

1/2 (top)
1/2 (bottom)

2 + Salt, Pepper, Herbs, Spices

3 (stir with spoon)

visit: www.stargoldthefoodfairy.com or www.stargoldfoundation.org

45

Iron Water
for those who need extra iron in their diet

Iron is an essential mineral with many important roles, mainly needed to transport oxygen to the brain and muscles. Iron deficiency is the most common and widespread nutritional disorder in the world and can lead to developmental delays in growing children. Iron is present in both animal products and plant foods but plant-based iron is not as readily available for absorption by the digestive system.

Here are recommended daily intakes based on your child's age:

Age	Male	Female
7-12 months	11 mg	11mg
1-3 years	7 mg	7 mg
4-8 years	10 mg	10 mg
9-13 years	8 mg	11 mg
14-18 years	8 mg	15 mg

Meet your child's iron needs through one of the following:
- Consumption of iron-rich foods such as meat, fish, eggs, legumes (beans, lentils), tofu, spinach; Include vitamin C rich foods (oranges, apples, tomatoes) to increase its absorption
- Daily iron supplementation
- Use Lucky Iron Fish in daily cooking*

https://ca.luckyironfish.com
*The Lucky Iron Fish releases 7 mg of bioavailable iron per use

Stargold's No-Recipe Recipes

Iron Water
for those who need extra iron in their diet

1 Wash Lucky Iron Fish

2 3 drops or — Add Lucky Iron Fish

Water 1 litre

LUCKY IRON FISH
luckyironfish.com

3 boil 10 min

4 Remove Lucky Iron Fish and cool water

5 1 cup Juice*

6 Enjoy!

*Juice: orange, pineapple, apple, cranberry, grapefruit, starfruit, etc.

visit: www.stargoldthefoodfairy.com or www.stargoldfoundation.org

47

Stargold's Pyramid
Nutrition Guide

**Balanced Eating
Mediterranean Food Pyramid**

Canada's Food Guide
Stargold's Plate

1/2 plate – Vegetables
1/4 plate – Protein
1/4 plate – Grains

Stargold the Food Fairy
by Claudia Lemay, RD

Word Finder

M	I	N	E	R	A	L	S	S	O	Y	L	I	M	A	F
V	E	G	E	T	A	B	L	E	S	B	F	U	X	O	R
I	I	A	S	L	I	O	W	S	E	R	S	O	O	E	U
T	C	N	T	B	U	N	I	A	A	C	R	D	B	L	I
A	U	T	B	A	D	E	N	M	L	A	F	O	H	N	T
M	L	I	E	E	L	S	E	E	N	A	U	R	C	O	S
I	D	O	L	H	R	T	S	G	I	P	I	C	N	I	C
N	L	X	P	S	H	R	E	R	P	E	A	N	U	T	O
S	O	I	P	K	T	N	Y	R	I	A	D	K	L	I	M
A	G	D	A	C	L	I	G	A	N	S	E	N	U	R	P
P	R	A	E	I	A	S	R	R	N	A	S	O	U	T	U
P	A	N	N	R	E	I	E	A	A	A	T	L	S	U	T
L	T	T	I	B	H	A	N	E	G	I	N	I	O	N	E
E	S	S	P	E	A	R	E	G	G	E	N	A	V	O	R
S	F	I	S	H	C	A	N	I	P	S	M	S	B	E	T
S	E	O	T	A	M	O	T	C	A	R	R	O	T	S	S

FIND THE WORDS IN THE TABLE ABOVE TO DISCOVER LUCIE'S SPECIAL MAGICAL MESSAGE FOR YOU WITH THE LEFTOVER LETTERS.

MEAT ALTERNATIVES	CARROTS	FAMILY	OMEGA	RAISIN	PICNIC
MILK DAIRY	SPINACH	ORANGE	PINEAPPLE	SESAME	GRAINS
ENERGY	FRUITS	BONES	PEANUT	HEALTH	BRICKS
FOOD FAIRY	COMPUTER	PEAR	LUNCHBOX	EGG	FRAME
VITAMINS	PRUNES	LUCIE	ANTIOXIDANTS	BERRY	BANANA
APPLES	TOOLS	STARGOLD	MINERALS	BEANS	MUSCLES
TOMATOES	NUTRITION	OILS	VEGETABLES	SOY	FISH

Illustrations by Chris Hamilton

Learn more from Stargold at
www.stargoldthefoodfairy.com

Stargold Games

When you drink pop, you really are drinking candy!

Draw connecting lines for the amount of sugar you think is in each drink below.

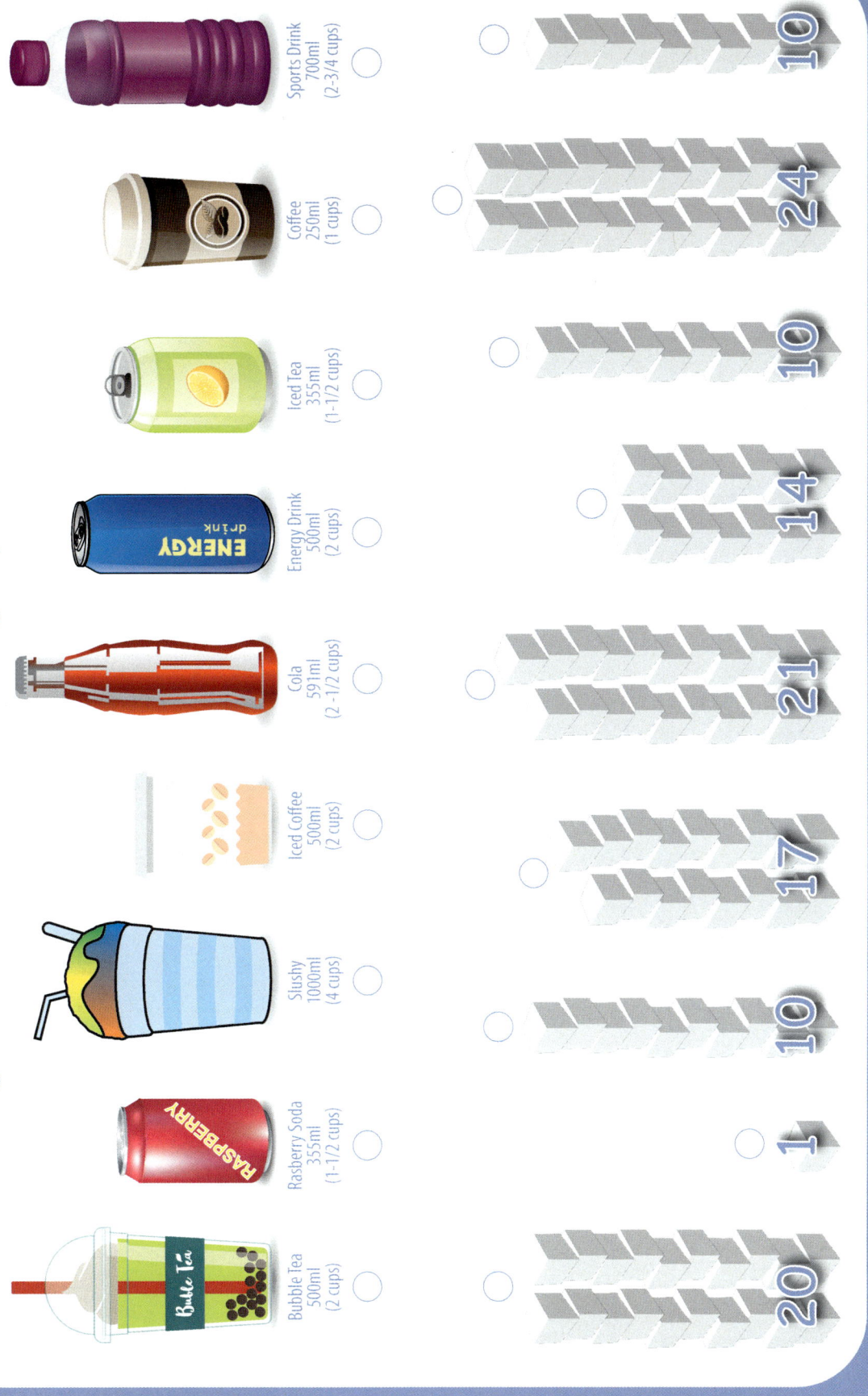

Drink	Sugar cubes
Sports Drink 700ml (2-3/4 cups)	10
Coffee 250ml (1 cups)	24
Iced Tea 355ml (1-1/2 cups)	10
Energy Drink 500ml (2 cups)	14
Cola 591ml (2-1/2 cups)	21
Iced Coffee 500ml (2 cups)	17
Slushy 1000ml (4 cups)	10
Rasberry Soda 355ml (1-1/2 cups)	1
Bubble Tea 500ml (2 cups)	20

The amount of sugar in these drinks varies by product and choice. 1 sugar cube = approximately 1 teaspoon of sugar

Answers: Bubble Tea-21 Rasberry Soda-10 Slushy-24 Iced Coffee-20 Cola-17 Energy Drink-14 Iced Tea-10 Coffee-1 Sports Drink-10

www.stargoldthefoodfairy.com

51

Stargold's Food Chart

Whole Grains = (girl playing soccer) = (lunchbox and toolbox)

Protein Foods = (strong kids) = (construction/building)

Fruits & Vegetables = Free radical / Antioxidant / Cell = (defeating monster)

Calcium-Rich Foods = (skeleton) = (house frame)

Healthy Oils & Fats = (brain) = (picture/movers)

Learn more from Stargold at
www.stargoldthefoodfairy.com

Illustrated by Chris Hamilton

Stargold's Food Guide

Healthy Oils & Fats

Protein Foods

Calcium-Rich Foods

Fruits & Vegetables

Whole Grains

Learn more from Stargold at
www.stargoldthefoodfairy.com

Illustrated by Chris Hamilton

Stargold the Food Fairy

by Claudia Lemay, RD

55

Stargold the Food Fairy
by Claudia Lemay, RD

An exciting adventure to illustrate the importance of nutrition to children.

Illustration by Chris Hamilton

Learn More from Stargold at
www.stargoldthefoodfairy.com

56

Stargold
the
Food Fairy
by Claudia Lemay, RD

Lucie

An exciting adventure to illustrate the importance of nutrition to children.

Learn More from Stargold at
www.stargoldthefoodfairy.com

Illustration by Chris Hamilton

Claudia Lemay, RD
Author

Claudia Lemay resides in Surrey, British Columbia, Canada with her husband, two kids and many pets. She works in private practice as a clinical dietitian. Claudia also created the program Eat.Go.Grow!, a summer camp for children that encourages healthy nutrition and physical activity.

To learn more about Stargold and healthy nutrition for children, or to find out how to order educational posters or this story in a teacher's presentation version, please visit www.stargoldthefoodfairy.com.

Illustrated by

Chris Hamilton    Chris Kielesinski

Manufactured by Amazon.ca
Bolton, ON